THEORY OF NON-HETEROSEXUAL EXISTENCE

One Man's Point of View About Human Nature

VERNON WATTS

Theory of Non-Heterosexual Existence

Copyright © 2021

Vernon Watts

All rights reserved First Edition

Acknowledgements

I want to first thank my Heavenly Father, Yahweh, who has always been with me and placed this concept in my heart for some reason I'm still not sure of. Thanks to my loving dad, Leo Watts, and my loving mom, Dora Watts, for instilling an inspirational foundation of the truth in my life. They both are with the Most High Yahweh now; how deeply do I miss them? There are no words. My dad's motto was "Son, own your own everything." My mom's motto was "Go with God (Elohim) and let Him bless you." Today, I'm still seeking to achieve both mottos. To Tiana, David, and Manwell, my beloved children who always encourage me to press forward with perspectives that you wouldn't hear from other people. To my soulmate, Nanette Weeks, who guided me through word analogy and allegory. To the Watts family who provided me with insight, love, and an ear into several views of this book. To Spark Imagination Publishing for believing in me, and the concept of this theory. Many thanks to you.

Table of Contents

Introduction

While this is a fictional book, it has its roots in reality. It features scriptural context and biblical verses to look up, as well as a few well-known authors specializing in psychology. This book is written to uncover the contrasting nature of gay people and heterosexuals. I attempted to probe the thoughts, feelings, and spiritual influences concerning a more excellent way to live with one another and continue the legacy of mankind "or not." I will point out the reasons why according to the scriptures, that the mind, our thoughts, and our inner spirit dictates how humans choose to live. Also, to prove that a lifestyle isn't ordered by other people, a gene, bloodline, or a deity; it's ordered by your own will. I never wanted to write this book; like Jonah (in the Bible), I ran away from doing so, for five years. Was I swallowed up by a big fish or whale? Heavens no!

But still, I was compelled to write this book against my own will. In the end, the Heavenly Father's "will" must triumph over mine.

This book is very controversial, and in some cases, abrasive to the readers because it touches on religion, the spiritual realm, racial conquest, gay and human rights. When I first started writing this book, I was very hard in my way of expressing some of the topics. But years later, as I continued writing this book, and as I listened to the Set Aside Spirit (Ruach) tell me how to be more subtle in my approach when conveying what messages would be appropriate, I just listened and learned.

I pray that the readers find interest in the "Theory of Non-Heterosexual Existence" thoughtful and intriguing to say the least. Also, let us learn how to treat one another with respect and equality until the day comes when there will be no need to try so hard. The way has already been revealed to us, we just haven't the Kingdom of Peace on earth yet. Enjoy!

Chapter One

The First Record

I was driving down the street one sunny partly clouded day in Dallas, Texas. I passed by many schools along the way to work, just like most people do on any given day of the week. But I noticed as it were, something quite extraordinary walking to school, although some of them were being dropped off by parents or guardians, "the children." I thought to myself, I wonder what morals children are being taught in school these days, as the kids ran freely laughing and talking to one another all the way into the school building. I smiled because I was just like them once upon a time, but we'll get back to the children in a later chapter.

The first time I heard the words "homosexual" and "lesbian," I was around eight years old. People had harsh words for them on the streets of Dallas, and I'm sure other cities around the world did also. People spoke of words like "muff diver," "faggot," "punks," "sissy," "bush," "queer," "booty bandit," and many other worst semantics commonly used back in the nineteenth century and throughout (and not limited to) the nineteen twenties, thirties and continued through the nineteen seventies and eighties.

The word "gay" meant happy go lucky or being keenly alive and exuberant, at least that's the way people in the civilized world, Noah Webster dictionary defined the word back then. There was no sexual intent behind the word gay, neither were there any gender implications, or content of sex in the meaning of the word gay listed in the early dictionaries of the 1700th, 1800th, and early 1900th century editions.

That was forever changed by this generation. By the way, all humans could be subject to feeling gay at any fleeting moment back then, and even today, if the word still lived up to its "original creed" because being gay to all humans was simply a good, happy go lucky feeling. It is common to feel a moment of exuberance because you were blessed with good fortune, or had a child, or finally got that degree, or any wonderful fulfillment or achievement, which made you feel alive again.

My oh my! How words can change from one generation to the next, from one meaning to another, just to fit a notion, a cause, or a category. Business used to be forged by a handshake and a word i.e. "My word is bond." Now it is more like, my word is "dung" because people today don't give a damn about how precious the meaning of words are. The meaning of words today changes like the wind, so what are we talking about, and what are we trying to convey when we talk to one another?

That is why the followers of Yahushua, love the Scriptures so much because it's so refreshing to the soul and spirit to know that the Word of Yahushua stays the same yesterday, today, and forever (Hebrews 13:8-9).

The first introduction to the word "homosexual" in America was around 1870. But when I searched certain books and the internet for an explanation for the lapses of time in translation to the English vocabulary, needless to say, I found several versions that provided some good explanations. But generally, most translations claimed it derived from the West Germanic language, which originated from the Anglo-Frisian dialects brought to Britain in the mid-fifth to the seventh centuries. But then it would have sounded more like 'homosexuelle.'

But for the sake of 'NOT' producing volumes of the "Theory of Non-Heterosexual Existence," there was one explanation I think you will love as much as I do, so here we go. I quote the author Richard Von Krafft-Ebing concerning the modern notion of sexuality that took shape at the end of the nineteenth century on this subject. "This modernization" of sexuality was intricately linked to the recognition of sexual diversity," as it was articulated in the medical psychiatric understanding, unquote. But at that time, it was labeled as sexual perversion and immoral because homosexuality and lesbianism were not considered normal human behavior by any Nations, Governments, Cities or Communities.

Later in the eighteen seventies, psychiatrists shifted the focus from immoral acts to (a temporary deviation from the norm) an innate morbid condition if you would. In the late nineteenth century, several psychiatrists collected and published even more data concerning case studies of homosexual practices that led to some historically concentrated documentation about homosexuality. They classified their works as a wide range of understandings, including the most popular ones classified as deviant sexual behaviors, mental disorder, and sexual perversion to name a few. The doctors listed in this book are public knowledge, which is easily traced, and readily available for consumption.

By the way, their conclusions led to the emergence of medical sexology therapy, in which most procedures were designed to show how the homosexual condition could be discussed, diagnosed, treated, and cured. No treatment was forced on any patient; they were all willing participants.

But Richard Von Krafft-Ebing offered a new perspective on homosexuality, not so much on lesbianism. He elaborated on a shift from a psychiatric perspective to more of a derived episodic symptom of mental disorder, based on a medical approach. He also considered it was merely "sexual perversion," but he had other thoughts about sex that brought about the integral urge in some people who accept continuous homosexual thoughts and the instinct to act upon them.

Krafft-Ebing was a major influence on some of the most prominent psychiatrists of the late 19th century, after more than 175 case studies through the years, ranging from 1846 to 1870. But in 1889, Krafft-Ebing became Chair of Psychiatry at the University of Vienna where he met and befriended Sigmund Freud. Krafft-Ebing's case studies were written well before Sigmund Freud had expressed similar views in 1905 with his (world-famous three essays) Theory of Sexuality. The word 'homosexual' was first used around 1892 in the

English translation of Richard Von Krafft-Ebing's "Psychopathia Sexualism," which was an enormously popular reference work in Germany on sexual perversions that first appeared in 1886. This is also public knowledge.

Richard Von Krafft-Ebing worked on this subject, and many others were printed and reprinted for years. By the way, Albert Moll (1862-1939), Sigmund Freud (1856-1939), Magnus Hirschfeld (1868-1935), even the Italian Physician, Psychiatrist, and writer, Paolo Mantegazza, and many others have concluded homosexuality to be a "mental disorder" or some form of disorder, nevertheless. Were they wrong?

Homosexual (adj.) in 1892, C.G. Chaddock's translation of Krafft-Ebing's Psychopathia, Sexualism from German languish (in both male and female studies) to the English word homo, was a combination of the Greek word homos (which means the "same"). You can search the Latin word homo-based on sexuality in the Greek vocabulary for more insight. Homosexual is a clinical hybrid word, but homogeny has been suggested as a substitute for homosexual by Havelock Ellis "studies in Psychology" in 1897. Sexual inversion was suggested in 1883 and was also offered in an earlier English clinical term, but it didn't gain appeal from the masses. By 1895, sexual inversion was recorded in technical terms, meaning either male or female, but in its non-technical terms, the use of the words almost always referred to a male-on-male sexual act. The slang word for homosexual was shortened on the streets of America, around 1929, to homo. I'm merely pointing out the views of these well-known historic doctors' studies and understandings of the gay lifestyle and the words associated with them. Don't stick a knife in my back yet.

But before all these well-known accredited people listed in this book, and all the case studies of gay individuals who also wanted to know why they felt an attraction to the same sex, before these doctors took the responsibility to investigate studies like this, and thousands of years before we coined the phrase "same-sex partners," the term used to describe homosexual acts was called "sodomy," and those who engaged in the act were called "sodomites." We will get back to them later. In the 'roaring twenties,' America placed a ban on booze, and "Prohibition" was born. So, gangsters who were always looking for a way to make a quick buck, went underground to begin opening speakeasies in New York, most notably between 45th and 52nd street, and other cities.

Gangsters saw a way to make big money from people that didn't have a place to party with other people that enjoyed same-sex entertainment. So began the "Pansy Craze" nightclubs and cabarets like the ones in Chicago, Illinois, and on the streets of many cities in the U.S. and abroad. Like the ones in Europe, Germany, but here in America, notably on Wabash Ave. and 15th street of Chicago. It has been recorded that the clubs stayed packed, and Al Capone and company made over 13 million dollars each year off regular customers, booze, and homosexual entertainers.

Many gay entertainers gathered in cities like San Francisco, Chicago, and New York clubs called "pansy parlors," but when Prohibition was repealed in 1933, almost all of the pansy clubs went out of business or became less attractive to business owners.

When there was no backing for profits, many high-profile gay entertainers went to mainstream radio, TV, and touring. Gangsters turned their attention elsewhere, mainly toward labor racketeering and gambling interest. Now, fast forward to a period in our society between 1940 to 1970, there has been very little progress in the homosexual community. Back then people felt being a homosexual or lesbian was against the order of mankind, the human anatomy, against the morality of being a civilized human, and more importantly, against the word of the Highest Yahweh as a whole.

Homosexuals went into the closet because most people gave paused to you if you were found to be a man or a woman who preferred the same-sex partner; you also would be subjected to reliquaries, being talked down to badly, picked on, hurt badly, or worse. In the sixties, things started to change a little, and with that change, guys like Little Richard, Liberace, and Rock Hudson among others, came on the scene and lit up the world stage for all to see.

Homosexuals in the regular neighborhoods remained in the closet for fear of reprisals, and it helped that many of their family and friends didn't know that they were homosexuals. But who are they if they are not showing who they are? If someone were to walk up to you and ask you this question, "Who are you?" What would your answer be? If you are gay and someone asks you that question, your response certainly wouldn't be, "I am gay." If you are heterosexual, surely your answer wouldn't be I am heterosexual. Some of you readers know the answer to that question already, but many of you still, after all these years on earth cannot give a definitive answer. So, who are you?

Since earthly questions are meant to be answered in a precise manner, take the time to know it. Let's look at a married couple, who has been together for forty, fifty, sixty years or more. If someone were to ask them that old proverb, "How did you guys manage to stay together all of these years?" The answer would no doubt be, "Here is where I want to be" or "I can't imagine myself anywhere else nor with anybody else."

Long-lasting marriages have found the secret of the phrase "For better or for worse" and that secret is "Here is where I wanted to be." Everybody knows that when you are getting married, you plan this great big day of celebration with friends and family, you hire a pastor to make it official between you and your wife. After the pastor has given many words of encouragement and offered up comfort of 'forever togetherness,' the pastor concludes the speech by saying something like this, "By the power invested in me, and before God almighty, I pronounce you man and wife." That doesn't ensure a long-lasting marriage. Although some choose to elope, running glazy eyed down to the county courthouse with that almighty gold diamond ring to finalize the union. After the glitz and glamor wears off, you soon find yourself thinking that the marriage certificate and wedding ring cannot keep your marriage from falling apart, but there's still hope for you if you can keep locked in your heart, and live life by (the covenant) these few historic questions, "Where do I want to be" and "Who am I?"

Chapter Two

The Gay Struggle for Acceptance

Gay activists had to link themselves to a struggle of epic proportion, so they chose the struggle of the black (Hebrew) race in America. They chose the time of slavery, and later during the civil rights movement in the sixties, to be their platform so that people around the world could see that they were being treated the same way as our so-called African ancestors were treated back then. But I'm totally confused about the gay struggle striving for acceptance being remotely close to, or even on a small scale as the black person's struggle for equality. The degree of lost property and land, the horrors, murders, rape, and systemic racism of black people around the globe, and what we had to endure during hundreds of years of degradation, even today, is without question, historically horrific on an epic scale.

I don't want to get into the black (Hebrew) American's history too deeply to prove a point, but I will say this one thing, be careful using the black race as a platform for the gay struggles because it might backfire against your movement and your personal struggles for equal rights. They didn't march for "freedom" of being born black, so it wasn't an internal conflict with society; it was and still is an external battle with white society's acceptance of black people's right to live as any man does, their right to pursue their hopes and dreams, and the struggles we have with the white society's views about African descendants around the world being viewed as genetically and intellectually inferior. By the way, it was never written that being born black was an abomination, nor is being negro (original Hebrews) a conflict with Yahweh's law and purpose for humanity.

Back to the gay struggle, after Sodom and Gomorra, homosexuals chose to stay in the closet if you would, in other words, they stayed quiet, and sault no attention to be paid to themselves for fear of reprisals. They found that being a homosexual man or a lesbian, you could move among the people unnoticed, that's if you didn't give any indication that you were indeed a lover of the same sex. After all, none would be the wiser unless you showed your hand because your anatomy can't give you away, but your body language could.

Gangsters kept it going for as long as they could until they got caught, or laws became softer on issues like liquor and gambling. The pressure of society broke down the walls to accept boozing citizens, and the law agreed with their agenda. (I'm going somewhere with this, so stay with me).

During the 1940s and throughout the 1960s, again there had been very little progress in the homosexual community because, during that period in our society, people felt like if you were a homosexual or lesbian, it was a sin against Yahweh and humanity. After WWII, being a homosexual was viewed as a sign of weakness and a mental issue in America and abroad.

However, during this time frame, a derogatory word emerged from out of Europe to identify homosexual people, this term being "Fag."

This term became very popular. Obviously, the word fag or faggot is a person puffing on a cigar or cigarette to yield its content of vapor or smoke down their throat while blowing some of it out through their mouth or nose. This derogatory term, as well as the others mentioned in the earlier chapter remained popular until a beautiful, sweet, nice word died and was buried. Then it rose again from the dead and became something to describe a sexual act between two people with the same anatomy, and it will never again be used to describe its original meaning again.

That word is gay.

The gay community had to change their identity to suit the populous and themselves with a friendlier view of homosexuals and lesbians. Knowing this, they chose a common word that is safer, milder, and softer to describe both homosexuals and lesbians. But before then, the word gay was commonly used in songs and speeches from the earlier years. All the songs written using the word gay throughout the 1800s until about 1970, the word gay had no sexual implications behind it. Ultimately, the word gay stopped being used in common everyday songs and conversations to describe a feeling of happiness and of a carefree, exuberant feeling, simply because of what it represents today. The original meaning of the word gay in conversations and in songs is dead.

Words are very important to mankind. It's paramount to the world to communicate all sorts of intelligent understandings and complex mathematic explanations. If words keep dying and changing to mean something totally different, then how can we communicate effectively?

Here are some words that are under attack as I write this book: family, man, woman, boy, girl, sister, brother, mother, father, marriage. What is right? What is wrong, good, evil? What is a baby? What is the truth? What is a lie? What is a person? And many others. All of these words will die soon, and they will be raised up again and mean nothing that we know them to mean today. Wake Up People! This is not by accident.

As was stated in the early chapter, there were kings who were gay or "wicked" or were all about that lifestyle. They ruled over an entire providence, we're witnessing (Jude 1:7) happening again today. Some of their names were: Be`ra King of Sodom and Bir`sha King of Gomorrah, some of the surrounding cities were Shi'nad King of Ad'mam, Shem-e'ber King of Ze-boi'im, King Zoar of the providence of Bela, including many other kings of the surrounding cities of Sid'dim located near the Dead Salt Sea (Genesis 14:2-3 and Genesis 19:1-25). These cities mentioned here might not mean much to you now but allow me to bring these cities back to life for your visual consumption, then maybe you can grasp the carnage. I'm from Dallas, Texas, so the size of Sodom and Gomorrah puts me in memory, (geographically speaking) of the Dallas, Fort Worth Metroplex, with its nearly 7,233,323 million people.

Here are some of the surrounding cities around the DFW Metroplex: Arlington, Irving, Plano, Richardson, Garland, Mesquite, Louisville, Desoto, Red Oak, Duncanville, Oak Cliff, Frisco, and a host of other cities. What if we suffered the same fate, all these cities would be wiped off the Texas map forever and never inhabited again. Other places come to mind also, like the Twin cities Minneapolis, Saint Paul in Minnesota, Kansas City, Kansas and Kansas City, Missouri, and all the cities surround them are great in the number of people who live there. Imagine all these cities wiped out in one day.

When you see the Sodom and Gomorrah account from a biblical standpoint, brought back to life, as seen in everyday light, it gives you a different visual into how great of a loss to mankind it was. People pleasers can be fatal to us if we don't take seriously, the laws given by Yahweh.

Please note that in Genesis chapter (19,4-5) the men in Sodom, both young and old men were trying to "rape" the Angels sent from Yahweh despite Lot offering up his two virgin daughters, to please their sexual appetite. But they had no desire for women, instead, they tried to force their way into Lot's home for the men who happened to be Angels in the form of man.

Isn't it true that the pleasure zone of a woman includes anal and mouth entry? I'm just saying. It's been said that "a mind is a terrible thing to waste," but I ask you, what are the controlling factors of the mind in humans? The body is simply a tool to do the will of the soul and spirit or the will (mind) of oneself. The body is in constant conflict with the soul and spirit. The body always wants all sorts of things, like a little child throwing a temper tantrum. Therefore, it must be kept under control by the soul and the spirit. Like that old Negro spiritual states, "You better check yourself, before you wreck yourself."

I'm making a little pun here, but it's a lesson to be learned by Snoop's statement, nonetheless. The body is so selfish and conning; it wants its way all the time, no matter if it's the right desire or the wrong desire; for instance, you may feel passion for someone else's wife, husband, or possessions, or a part in a play that wasn't meant for you, or an unwarranted hatred of a people you don't even know, your flesh just always want to do things selfishly. Yahweh calls this type of lifestyle, living in the flesh and not living according to the spirit. For those of you who live in the flesh, it impossible to please your Heavenly Father Yah, neither are they a child of the Most High Yahweh, so stop practicing desires of the fleshly behavior (Romans 8:4-9).

The soul of mankind harbors its own free will, conscience, and character. The understanding of a person who lives a lifestyle that pleases Yahweh, even while no one is around or watching, is called a true child of Yahweh. But the soul can make the body do some evil, crazy, wicked things, whether there's anyone around to witness it or not. The body can't control the soul; the soul is in control of the body to do its desires. The spirit is the breath of life (Genesis 2:7) that Yahweh gave to us in order to fellowship with him on a personal level, but because he gave us free "will," or some would say freedom to "choose" not to have a relationship with the Heavenly Father, we do our own thing.

Also, you can "choose" to have a relationship with Baal, Satan which will cause you to do the will of Satan. So, you can serve the Spirit of Yahweh or the spirit of Satan. It's your choice how to balance your body, soul, and spirit (Joshua 24:14-15). Back to the theory, it's been a long battle between society's views of morality and gay people's views of morality, but in some circles of society, doors have been opened to accept the gay lifestyle as normal behavior, that's a huge milestone. Now we can see things are turning around for our gay earthen brothers and sisters.

The movement into everyday society has increased immensely, like in the field of teaching our children, infiltrating mainstream pageants that were originally set up for biologically born women.

Adopting children as a two father or a two-mother family setting, having gay churches, giving into marriage, and lobbying for more changes that only fit how gay people see the world regardless of society's approval of it or not. Gay lobbyists are in the governmental branches.

With the government on their side, they can force companies, institutions, pageant systems, schools, and

19

churches, yes churches, to accept gay rights or be bullied or punished if they go against gay wishes.

All these institutions are being targeted by the gay community and the government if they won't accept the gay lifestyle as normal; any institution can be bullied or sued by gay rights activists for sexual discrimination. Could you have imagined that sexual preference would become more important in our society than the U.S. Constitution and biblical principle set by Yahweh which was written thousands of years ago for the preservation of mankind? Not to be concerned about this movement people, for it will profit them nothing who lives in fleshly lawlessness and immorality. Because of this behavior, Yahweh gave some warning to those who deny and reject His anointed ones (Jude 1:3-4), He will not spear you if you don't repent and turn back to Him, for He didn't spare the Angels that fell from Heaven nor the first earth from the flood (II Peter 2:4-6).

Let me be the first to say this, "Congratulations gay community," you have reached "Sodom and Gomorrah status."

Evil spirits are real and can be cast out of us (Matthew 8:29). Let him who have an ear, hear what the Word of the Yahshua is saying today. If you're gay, then stay gay, and if you aren't, then remain as you are. Yahushua said, every tree (spirit of the body) that bears 'not' good fruits (Spiritual peace, self-control, chastity, kindness, etc.) Not Earthly weak false peace, kindness, control, chastity, etc. Those of you who do your 'own will' and do not the 'will' of our Savior Yahushua Ha Mashiach (The Messiah) will be cut off and cast into the fire (Matthew 7:19-23).

Yahuah, the same one who displayed a more excellent lifestyle while He was on this earth, is the same one we should mimic. So, if any gay person thinks they're a follower of the Son of the Most High, please seek the Holy Word of Yahweh and mimic His Son's lifestyle first, then try to match your lifestyle to the Heavenly Savior, or at least the disciples who were sent to share the Holy Scriptures to the world. Any lifestyle that doesn't mimic the lifestyle of Yahuah (some call Jesus) Your life must be representative of The Son, while you're yet in your present body. A perfect lifestyle is one who's sacrifice (give up, stop, cease or destroy) pleasures to the 'will' of your Heavenly Farther so that He can redeem your soul back to its original place with Him.

That's the main reason our Heavenly Father sent His Son to earth as the "Son of man" (Yahweh is with us). It would be a beautiful thing if you go back to the scriptures and take the time to follow the Commandments, Laws, Statues of the Most High. Don't just read the scriptures, do them. If we remain in the lifestyle that we're in without repentance and sacrifice, according to the Word of our Heavenly Savior, things won't end quite well for heterosexuals, nor for homosexuals.

Let's continue, the gay community has made great strides in politics, directing mainstream movies, government agencies, public school systems, sports, fire departments, childcare agencies, and other prominent agencies with authority positions so that they can make the world in their image and become more accepted by the masses.

That's a long way from being subjected to psychiatric treatment, to becoming acceptable as a normal everyday lifestyle. Again congratulations, you have entered the door of Sodom and Gomorrah. For it is written, as it was in the days of Noah, so it will be before the return of the Most High Son Yahushua. Matthew 24:37-39, this is a sign from the Most High to the world and His chosen people today, that when things mimic the days of Lot, destruction will soon follow (Luke 17:25-30) and lastly, in the book of (Jude 1:7-8). The Heavenly Father gave a warning to people of this age who practice unnatural acts as they did in Sodom and Gomorrah and reject His warnings. The whole earth will suffer greatly because governments made it a right to do so, and said in their hearts, Yahweh can't do anything about it.

Chapter Three

Yahweh's Law of Morality

For those of you who don't respect or believe in the word of Yahweh, pay close attention to what is written here; you will learn something you may not have known nor otherwise understood. This is how Yahweh views homosexuality as it pertains to the Holy scriptures. Incidentally, "the truths you'll learn in this chapter about morality should be very beneficial to how you view your own life choices from this day forward."

Let's start at the beginning. Yahweh created men and women to complement each other in every way, and Yahweh said to them, "be fruitful and multiply, and replenish the Earth" (Genesis 1:26-28), and in the New Testament, St. John 1:1-14). These scriptures have given us a clear and precise picture of the arrival of man on earth. Also, Genesis 1:28 depicts the first time we were given a commandment from our Heavenly Father to procreate, a natural desire for sex between man and woman. No other sexual desires were given by Yahweh. Our Heavenly Father didn't say, "be fruitful and multiply" as a suggestion; it was the first commandment given to us, which in elementary terms means, go reproduce yourselves. The replacement of dinosaurs ushered in a better, more personal relationship with Yahweh that dinosaurs couldn't ever achieve.

Mankind was given the authority to have a more kindred spirit with Yahweh, a clear personal understanding which comes from a healthy fear of the Most High Yah (Self Existing One) and a closer connection to the very essence of Yahweh. I believe that the real truth about dinosaurs is to give us a glimpse of just how awesome and powerful our Creator really is. The fear (respect) of Yahweh is the beginning of knowledge (Proverbs 9:10 and Proverbs 1:7). His first command was for us to be fruitful and multiply, we did that. After mankind populated the earth or as our gay counterparts would say, after the breeders populated the earth, there was a law of morality given to mankind from the Most High (not from me), and that law stated that no man shall have sex with another man, and likewise, no woman shall have sex with another woman, nor with animals less the land vomit you out of it (Leviticus 18:22-30).

This is an abomination in the site of God (Leviticus 20:13) and to the land also. You will find all throughout the scriptures, that we as a people are in a direct relationship with the land which we live, eat, wash, play, and cultivate daily. So, as we sin against the Heavenly Father, our land will suffer too. By the way, although some of us love having a close relationship with Him, yet if we're living immorally in His sight, not in your best friend's sight, not in your family's sight, and not in the government's sight, do we dare the

Heavenly Father to visit us, while we're being rebellious and disobedient in His sight.

I say this to you all because people sometimes say the silliest things like, "Where is your Heavenly Father now, why doesn't He come down and show Himself face to face?" I can give you scripture after scripture of what happens when Yahweh visited mankind, when they were being rebellious like we are today.

So, if He punishes us as a nation for our transgressions against Him, He will also plague the very thing that we stand on every day, 'our land' (Leviticus 18:24-26). Practicing sin before Yahweh is deadly, and He showed us just how deadly He can be if we don't follow His instructions for the preservation of mankind and stay within the natural laws and heavenly statutes and ordinances (not mine) that He put in place. The same was in place on the first earth and the second earth. We, as humans, continue to learn and ponder about what brought about the destruction of these past worlds. Perhaps some of you readers haven't heard of what happened to the first and the second earth from a biblical standpoint.

The first earth, as far as mankind's knowledge of it, was destroyed by a catastrophic event, so the Most High had to restore the ecosystem back to its original state (Genesis 1:1-2). The sun was also destroyed, as well as the moons, along with the other stars in our universe. The earth became deformed and void of any kind of life. The dinosaurs that were created before mankind arrived were destroyed, and all the inhabitants of the sea, and yes, the entire microorganism died too.

What is really shown in the biblical text here is all life was destroyed, including the universe we now have the pleasure of enjoying; it did not exist in the manner you see it today because of the catastrophe. The earth is not billions of years old because time had not started yet. Allow me to let my imagination seek a possible understanding of what could have caused such a calamity. This is just my point of view as one who is part of the human race and one who align my thoughts with some of the scriptures of the Bible.

In the book of Revelation 4, 12: 7-9, evil angels were heralded down from heaven like great lightning bolts to the earth—Satan and his followers (Luke 10:17-18). Because of these scriptures, I can visualize these angels (ten times more powerful than the atomic bombs), falling with great force to the earth and the entire universe for that matter because it was one-third of the entire angelic forces of the Host of Heaven being cast out like lightning bolts.

Although no one on this earth knows (including me), the number of evil angels that were cast out of heaven, what we do know is that they are powerful beyond our own understanding. And when they fell throughout our universe and the earth, "They Didn't Die," they are still here, with orders from Satan (the father of rebellion), working to destroy our relationship with Yahweh.

In fact, some of them are so terrifying and detrimental to mankind, that they had to be chained up by "Abaddon," his name in Hebrew (Revelation 9:11), the king of demon slayers, "Apollyon" in Greek. By the way, Abaddon is not a demon, he's a destroyer of demons and those who worship demons.

You might say, why is this important to gay people and the readers of this book? (Matthew 10:28). Because if there's something out there that has the pleasure of destroying strong fallen angels' souls, how much more will they torture your wimpy butt and destroy your soul in the second death? I don't want to meet these powerful guardians of Yah. If one gets cast into the lake of fire which is the bottomless pit, you will have to deal with Abaddon (Revelation 9:1-11). I must state that old great American Urban philosophical warning "don't go there." I know, I am speaking of something you know not of. Keep reading please.

The second earth was destroyed by the Great Flood (Genesis 7:4-24). Noah, however, did not just gather animals two by two of its own breeds. He gathered seven by seven clean animals, and two by two, unclean animals (Genesis 7:2-3) because of the lawlessness and wickedness of mankind, who defied the order of Yah, but instead, they enjoyed whatever lifestyle and wicked 'thoughts' that came to their imagination. {By the way, there's clean and unclean people too} (John 13:11).

They did whatever they wanted to do, whenever they wanted to do it, as long as it was right in their own eyes to do so, every day. Unfortunately, for mankind, it was only perversion, hatred toward man and Yahweh. They reveled in wickedness all day, every day, with corruption and violence continually.

So, if a man wanted to rape his best friend's wife, sister,

or brother, it was ok in that crazy mixed- up world. If you wanted to steal another man's possession, kill whomever you wanted to, it was ok. Whatever man, woman, boy, or girl wanted to do, even defiling animals, the law of the land in that world was "if it feels good to you, do it." That is why it had to be destroyed (Genesis 6:5-7, 11-12). Yahushua said, "Whatever goes into a man is not necessarily evil because it just passes through the body and out, but whatever comes from the heart of a person can be evil, and that's what defiles a person" (Mark 7:18-23).

In fact, the lifestyle that they chose (on the second earth) was just fine with society's viewpoint of what they thought was life, and there were no consequences for their actions. So, someone may think this is right in my eyes, I don't care what's right in your eyes. Society's standard of what was righteous and what was wrong was entirely left up to one's own interpretation. They followed their own 'will,' not the will of Yahweh. Immorality and evil, murder, rape, witchcraft, drunkenness, all types of perversion, hatred, lovers of pleasure were normal to humans in that world. But people who practiced that lifestyle didn't inherit (live forever on) the second earth and shall not inherit the third earth, nor will they enter the Kingdom of the Most High (1 Corinthians 6:8-10).

Yahweh has not given us the spirit of fear, instead, He has given us the spirit of peace, love, and a sound mind (2 Timothy 1:7). That tells us, that our Heavenly Father has given us a mind of peace that is altogether different from the temporary peace of mind that you have here on earth. A peace of mind that transcends all human understanding (Philippians 4: 7) and His thoughts and ways are not like our thoughts and ways (Isaiah 55:8-9). His chosen lifestyle for us is a more excellent way than what we can choose for ourselves. "If we're willing," we can regain that Heavenly lifestyle.

The second earth had fallen far, far away from what was good and noble, it had to be destroyed. Our society today has become the same way, with compromise after compromise, acceptance after acceptance, until only evil every day, all day becomes the norm. The only difference between this world and the second world is that we still have pockets of morality left.

Despite the constant warning and crying out against such a lifestyle from Noah, the people wanted nothing to do with what Noah was teaching, nor what he was advocating; they thought he was outdated. To them, what Noah spoke of was just taboo and they poked fun at him and his family because of it.

Man disregarded Yahweh's principles for good, clean living and chose rather, to govern their own lifestyle. If we don't include Yahweh in our everyday lifestyle today, a worse thing will come upon us tomorrow. If we don't take heed to all the warning signs of this age, even the ones in this book, evil will overtake us continually (Genesis 6:5-7).

Question—can the church operate effectively under the rule of the state? The thief comes to kill, still, and destroy lives (John 10:10). If gay people want to be joined as life partners, let it take place at any venue in the United States.

But why is it important to the gay community to 'bully' the church into joining them and their partner for life. When churches reject to share your view of what marriage is, isn't it more pleasing for you to share your celebratory unions in a place that happily shares your views? I am sure there are many willing venues out there to accommodate your occasion, than venues that don't. Which is better? A woman walks into a lion's den at feeding time, or that same woman walks into her family dining room at feeding time? Which is better?

Incidentally, it's neither the church nor children of Yahweh's job to stand in the way of sinners, nor is it the job of the church to sit on any board or counsel to help any gay cause (Psalm 1:1). However, it is the church and the children of Yahweh's responsibility to be a beacon to guide the lost and confused, to understand what righteous and Holy is according to the Word of the Most High. But only the churches that are guided by Yahweh can achieve this. Keep in mind the followers of Yahuah will not be bullied nor intimidated by gangsters, hate groups, prostitutes, murderers, gays, nor the government. Let's find out what Sin really is.

Sin

First, let me share with you how sin entered into our lives (the world). When mankind first arrived on earth, there was no sin in mankind, and there was no sin being cultivated on earth by any animal, insect nor any other creatures. The world was perfect. Then Lucifer rebelled (sin) against the Heavenly Father and was kicked out fiercely and fell to earth where he remains today. (Revelation 12:7-12). Adam and Eve were placed in the Garden of Eden and Eve listened to the words of Lucifer (serpent) and rebelled (sin) against the Heavenly Father and was kicked out of the Garden of Eden (Genesis 3:1-6) and (Genesis 3:22-23). So here we are. The Word said we're all born in sin and shaped by iniquity (Psalm 51:5). So, we can see that anyone is capable of committing sin, followers of Yahweh and followers of Satan of course. Sin is in our bloodline, as I say today, it's in our DNA to sin, and that's so true because when Adam and Eve explored the opportunity to become a god (Genesis 3:4-5), sin happened. As you can clearly see, mankind wanted badly to become like Yah before the timeline that Yahweh had set. Selah

There is nothing wrong with wanting to become like Yahweh (Psalm 82:6-7), if you go about, it the right way (John 10:33-35), and the only way to become like Yah is through Yahuah (Son of Yah). Then and only then can you be called the sons and daughters of Yah (some call God). A righteous spirit is the opposite of a sinful spirit. Our Creator has a plan for you to become like Him. It was set up for you and from the foundation of the world, He made it possible. Adam and Eve went about it the wrong way; they disobeyed the commandment of Yahweh (Genesis 2:16-17) on their own quest to become a god (small 'g,' meaning impossible to rise above Yahweh).

Let me make a "funny" comment about the gods of this world, which some of you call yourselves. It's like an ant calling you over to your patio chair and wanting to have a sip of tea and crumpets with you and start a conversation about its place in your yard. To make this funny conversation even more insightful to you, you understand the ant's dialog, and the ant understands yours.

The ant starts out by saying, "Hi god of this yard, how are you this cool refreshing day? Let me say that I've been checking you out for a long time now, and I want all that you have in my possession. I want to control what you control. So, I've been thinking, studying you, reading what makes you tick, and I can respect your power and control. Sure, we had our differences over the centuries, I've invaded the picnics that you threw for the other gods in your domain, and you wiped out my whole mounds simply because I tasted your delicacies."

"Yes, it's true I bit your children and your dog for disturbing my mound, then you banished us from the mist of your yard with chemicals, including killing my queen!!, What's was that about? Well, today, I'm going to rise above you, and you will be subject to me and to my sibling, my ant mound will rise above your house, and you will go where I say you can go and do as I tell you to do. Starting today, when I bite you and your children, you will lay down and take it because, this is my decree over you, and I will reign over you and all the other gods you associate with from now on."

The man just looks at the ant, laughs, and then he laughs again and says, "Good luck with all of that ant." This is an example of what a god is in the eyes of the Most High Yahweh. So, you consider that the next time you proclaim that you're a god. You darn ant.

If we're born in sin, and shaped by the world system to sin, then what's the problem? Death, the laws, commandments, and statutes of Yahweh is the problem. What person that you know of can't die? (1 Corinthians 15:56). Sin is being disconnected from our Heavenly Father and transgressing the law; therefore, when we disobey His 'will' for our life choices and cling to our own life choices that's called rebellion. Sin is simply a singular act that we commit, and it has nothing to do with righteousness but has everything to do with the unrighteousness. We inherited from Adam and Eve, passed down to us from generations to generations, which goes against the laws of Yahshua (Romans 5:12-14). The unfortunate thing about this, is the wages of sin is death; I'm not talking about the first death, I'm referring to the second death (Romans 6:23).

People commit sin knowingly and unknowingly because some sins are taught by those who so call love you and they love the world, but the love of the Heavenly Father is not in them. When we commit sin, some of us will be chastised (corrected) for committing sin, and others will not be chastised because they "do not" belong to The Heavenly Father (Hebrews 12:6-8). We know committing sin is not the will of Yah, but our own will. Those that are led by the Ruach (set aside Spirit) knows what to do to be forgiven of their sins (which is repent). Others do not respect Yahweh nor ask for forgiveness. Yahweh's correction is a good thing; you should be happy that you receive correction from the Most High Yah. That way, you'll know that He still considers you his child, but you better repent (turn from practicing sin) never do it again.

Sinning

Sinning is the attitude of people who know what sin is, they know it is wrong to do it, and they can turn away from sinning but choose not to. They also know that there will be consequences if they are caught sinning, and they know it is against the will of the Almighty. They continue to give into sin and let it rule their mind and body even though the chains have been broken.

To them, it's the rush they get from doing something wrong because to the sinning group, being a good person is boring. Doing things, the right way is corny (1 John 3:4-10). They love living on the edge, constantly pushing the envelope to achieve a certain climax that they can't get from being content with what is honest, truthful, fair, and wise. They don't sympathize with people who don't drink to just get drunk and don't cuss with them. They're dumbfounded with people who won't engage in wrong doings with them, and they look at you as a wimp if you don't do what's in your nature to do, for so-called fun.

They're the ones who straddle the fence between serving Yahweh one day and serving Satan (gods) the next day. They're perfectly fine with that arrangement until reality sets in. These are the ones that the movie "Left Behind" was based on, the same will get caught up in the tribulation period (Revelation 11) if they don't stop the charade before it's too late.

Yes, they're the ones who go to church playing with fire, after sinning all night at the clubs and hotels. They hope to enjoy the pleasures of this world and heavenly rewards too. "NOT." The sinning group mostly knows the word of Yahuah but "no not" Him. They operate under the cloak of convenience. They aren't murderers, but if they caused someone to get killed because of their shenanigans, they'll feel bad for a minute, hopefully, some of them will turn from sinning for a while. You see, this group must be jolted from their wicked ways, like when the rooster comes home to roost, only then will they come back to the Most High Yah.

Sinner

The scriptures have a lot of good things to offer sinners because Yahuah came into the world, not for the righteous, but instead, He came just for the sinners, to redeem the sinners back to Him (Matthew 9:10-13 and John 3:16). Please, all of you sinners, take heed to these scriptures and repent because they're all about you being a lost group of people who needs to be reminded of who you are. Sinners live their lives without knowing the Savior. They don't pray, at least not with the righteous heart; even if a sinner prays, Yahweh wouldn't hear them (John 9:31 and Job 27:9).

Sinners don't believe you have to serve the Lord to be a good person.

They don't have any convictions of committing sin, nor do they have any remorse about being a sinner, nor any interest in knowing the Most High Yah. Have you ever heard that ignorance is bliss? That's the sinner. But beware! You will not escape Elohim's wrath (Romans 1, 18) So, one of his followers shows up and ask, "Do you know Yahuah?"

Sinners then after hearing the Word of Yahuah, must choose to believe it or not, no excuses are accepted after that because even Yahuah hung out with sinners to shine light on them and lead them out of darkness (Luke 15:2).

Living in Sin

The living in sin group is the worst group of all the sin groups. These people know that they are living in sin, they know that living in sin is against the righteousness of Yahweh and will fight tooth and nail to have the whole world live in sin with them. They will reject correction from anyone, any agency, any government, and that includes the Almighty. These people are hell-bent on living in sin; they're not content with just committing sin, but they desire sin over anything, (1 Peter 4:3-4), and that includes life itself.

They love it, embrace it, and can't live without it, sound familiar? Once you start accepting this type of sin in your life, it becomes very, very hard to overcome. This group has sold their own soul to do evil in the sight of Yahweh and man. They teach you things like, it's doesn't make you evil if you steal when you need to, there's no absolute right or wrong, abortion is a good convenient way to rid yourself of troubles, besides, it's your body. There's nothing wrong with having two men or two women in the role of a mother and father, what you don't know won't hurt you, I don't need Yahweh to be a good person. Lastly, my favorite, by the way, I won't compromise for anybody or anything, it's my life.

In conclusion, most sins can be forgiven if we repent of our transgressions. Living in sin is very devastating to your soul because again, this type of sin is hard to pull away from, especially if you've been in it for a long while now. Living in sin is not the same as being a sinner (not knowing Yahuah) or just committing a singular sin and asking for forgiveness because you felt convicted.

Most of all, the living in sin group is very hard to turn back to Yahweh because, in their hearts, they feel that there's no real need to be forgiven. They feel like Yahuah died for ALL sins, so what's the need to ask for forgiveness. What they don't know is, yes you are forgiven for all sins, but you must discontinue (repent) from committing the sins you are forgiven for (Acts 3:19). Also, you must work out your own salvation with fear and trembling daily (Philippians 2:12).

I've shared with you why all sins aren't the same and the last sin will prove it, (Matthew 12:31). But one sin group will never be forgiven, and that is the ones who blaspheme the Ruach (Holy Spirit). No, I will not tell you what blaspheming is, and no, I will not tell you how to do it because it's not good for man to know some things. Besides, if you don't know what it is, then maybe you won't do it, and if you have done it without knowing that devastating act, maybe just maybe, your punishment may be lighter. But if you have knowingly done this awful devastating thing, then "may Yahweh have mercy on the bottom and the top of your soul."

Allow me to address some online statements about our Savior.

I think it's very important to bring the truth to the hearts and souls of those who graciously weighed in about Yahweh, science, and the scriptures in the Bible on homosexual practice online. How gays should be viewed from the concept of being judged on sexual preferences. Even though most people do not want to hear the truth on this subject because the truth isn't popular, nor does it feel good to one's ego, or the psyche of the mind.

There are many buzz words and comments being tossed around in quotes today, as if they are stand-alone words and can't be explained, like "cherry-picking the scriptures," "don't judge me," "God made us this way," "Jesus didn't speak against homosexual practice," "God has forgiven our sins, "we now know more about homosexuals than the writers of the Bible," etc.

In the matter of Christianity, let me state for the record, I am not a Christian. I am a child of the Most High Yahweh. I used to be a Christian for many years until Christian became an Institution of money, power and of religious creeds. My faith is in Yahuah. Contrary to popular belief, Christianity was never meant to become a religion or a business, but that's what it is today. When the Romans conquered Jerusalem in 70 A.D, they forced the children of (Hebrews) Yahweh (some call God) along with the other gods that the Romans served, and later they called it Christianity.

Followers of Yahuah must leave behind their earthly lifestyle, deny themselves, take up their cross (Matthew 16:24-26), learn His way of living (Matthew 4:18-20 and Matthew 9:9). The followers of Yahuah use scriptures when faced with questions about life, especially when it pertains to spiritual matters. Because of this, the Holy Scriptures give us the answers we need.

I'll try to answer some of the comments previously stated by the gay community. By seeking Biblical context and methodology, you can clearly, rightfully divide the word and let the word of our Heavenly Father give an answer. The precepts upon precepts and concepts upon concepts, here a little, (Isaiah 8:10-12) there a little, until you can get a full understanding. By the way, all the writers of the Bible were led by the Ruach (Holy Spirit) "but you can't understand it or hear it?"

Because you don't have the Ruach inside you to teach you. So, it's easy to toss random words around.

For instance, the word "judge" had a different action attached to it back then, when it was spoken over 2000 years ago; "don't judge me." Believe me, you don't want that word to have the same "action" it meant back then, in today's world. Just to enlighten you about this biblical scripture; don't judge less ye be judged, with the same measure you judged (Matthew 7:1-2). The word "judge" today is a joke, compared to its original meaning.

Today, the word "judge" is likely to hold the same action as, "Don't criticize me." According to the Scriptures when it was written, a mob would grab you out of your home (John 8:3-11), take you out of the city, and "judge" you according to their culture.

Next, the mob would accuse you of a wrongdoing (in this case, being gay), then they would become your judge, and you would be "sentenced" by the community, then they would pronounce "judgment" on you and execute you, right then and there. Sometimes, depending on the sin you committed, they would execute your whole family as well. Now that's being judged.

By the way, stoning was the weapon of choice for judgment in those days. I laugh when I hear people say, don't judge me. No one uses this method nowadays. They use mercy today instead of stoning (James 2:12-13). Let me be clear, today you're not being judged because of your life choices. You're living the way you want to live. Whatever you decide to do on earth, please don't practice something that will dishonor Yahweh continuously (Proverbs 15:3-4).

Another comment you hear a lot from the gay community is, "Why single us out of all the rest of the transgressions committed by man?" Although it true that all have sinned and come short of the Glory of Yahweh.

But then murderers, fornicators, stealers, whoremongers, adulterers, rapist, worshipers of graven images, and many other sinners aren't trying to force their lifestyle upon the schools, churches, police departments, military, businesses, and any other entities for acceptance, the gay community is the only one. The door is open now for the others mentioned here to follow suit and they are hot on your skirt tail.

You brought yourself out so the world can discuss your plight. Most of the time, when there's a controversial movement or group of people forcing its way to the forefront, they get singled out. Let's take a look at what type of people Yahushua created and the lifestyle He commanded them to cultivate. So, in these verses, Genesis 2:21-24, Matthew 19:4-5, and Ephesians 5:31, and several other verses, we can clearly see that the creator ordained man and women to become one flesh in unity only. None of us would be here if we were born any other way, for that matter, without this rich desire to procreate, there would have been no need for sexual pleasure. In other words, no heterosexuals and no homosexuals would be here, including you.

The notion of being different from the way we were created is of our own doing. Our own body cries out to us what we are and what sexual partner our body type is perfectly fitted for, so we don't have to choose nor question if we're a man or a woman. Because of the definitive, scientific natural body anatomy, (Genesis 1:20-28) which shows us without question or confusion that all creation knows what they are. We have knowledge of our own anatomy that Yahushua created, however, I could think in my heart one day, I'm a dog, or a lion, or an eagle or a woman, and start practicing the lifestyle to become that which I feel I am.

By the way, there are people who feel they're indeed what I just described, look it up. As for sexual preference, I haven't seen any newborn babies coming out of the womb having sex yet, nor knowing what sex is, nor clinging to another newborn of the same sex for nourishment. Neither can any doctor on the face of this earth deliver a newborn baby and proclaim, "This one is gay."

Never had it been a time in history, where a human could hire a doctor to alter their anatomy to simulate what they 'feel' inside until now. Because no matter what you feel inside, or have doctors cut off or add to your body, which is unnatural construction, (Romans 1:26-27). All you would have accomplished by altering your natural body construction is to reject what Yahushua preferred you to be. However, if that's your goal, well destruction is around the corner.

Go ahead and say to yourself, I was born gay, I have more Y chromosomes than X chromosomes, I felt like a man all my life, and there's nothing wrong with me being gay. This is the real reason why gay people feel like they do, and why they desire the same-sex partners according to the biblical account (Romans 1:21-28). This scripture explains the real reason why you are gay. Let me say this to all of those who are reading these valuable principles from the word of Yahweh, He loves you and He doesn't want you to think He is against you, and I love you too. But some of you know you aren't who you say you are; you just don't know how to return back to your loving Father which is in Heaven. But the love of Yahweh can't save you from His wrath because you're rejecting the fact that His son died for your sins, so all He is waiting for is your "repentance."

Don't be ashamed to repent and turn from your ways and let Yahweh do the rest. You know you can do this. Are you sure you haven't fallen into the love of pleasure, wishes, and desires (2 Timothy 3:4)? If you just study what Yahweh said to you and study the books of the truth, it's easy to find your way home.

I know it's radical to think like this, but again, the fact that Yahuah loves you isn't going to save you from His wrath. Yahweh and the scriptures aren't there to hurt us, instead, they're here to help guide us back to Him. He will make you the best you, you can be, not science, not pastors, not me. Science is when human discovers what Yah already created and was already here, not what they created. Yahweh placed throughout the whole universe, untold secrets that humans can discover over ten thousand years of studies, scientists and doctors can't help you, but your Heavenly Father's Love will. It's all His design, not ours. Science and doctors are just a means to an end.

Yahweh has proven it by many former gay men and women throughout the years. I would venture to say that most of you readers know of someone in your own community that was considered gay but now is not. Speaking of being born of something, we all are born in sin and shape by iniquity (Psalm 51:5). Since we are born of the flesh, the world dictates to us that whichever way you choose to live is good inside our hearts or out. We know somethings are against the order of Yahweh, but it feels good. If you're born of the spirit and practice those things that the Most High Yah reveal to you, then your spirit wouldn't be ruled by the gods of pleasure, which is hell-bent on ruling your mind and body.

I heard a comedian say something to the fact of, Christians are so narrow-minded about gay people and what Christ cares about. He said the Ten Commandments didn't say anything about, man shall not have sex with man; women shall not have sex with women. So, it must not have been that important, right? Sometimes when you hear stuff like this, it sounds reasonable, doesn't it? but that which sounds reasonable has nothing to do with the "truth" the truth is there are more than ten commandments, and the truth is Yahweh said not to commit such acts within His commandments, Laws, under His statutes or ordinances. Always do those things that are good in His sight, what is noble in His eyes, what is kind to Him, what is honorable to Him, keep His morals and obey His Word. This is why He gave us a brain.

Since Yahweh gave us a brain, He thought that we would use it. But since we didn't use our own intellect in common matters, He allowed (at our request), kings to make rules, laws, and ordinances over us (1 Samuel 8:4-22) and kings and queens to rule over the providences. He gave us every chance to get it right. Scripture after scripture, He warned us of our pathetic views of what morality is. We didn't care, as long as we had our own morals to feed on.

That is why the Laws of Morality, ordinances, and statutes not to commit those actions, is clearly seen in Moses' writings (Leviticus 18:22-30). As Yahweh said, "Be ye separated from the world morals, don't be unequally yoked and touch not the unclean thing." If we can do this, then our Heavenly Father will receive us as His Sons and Daughters (II Corinthians 6:14-18 and Isaiah 52:11). For these are Babylonian practices.

Enough of this Biblical sharing, let's get to the real reason why I was compelled to write this book.

Chapter Four

A New Day

Well, let's just say the elusive gay gene took an interesting turn of events and every person being born from this day forward was gay. Since we know that gay people get repulsed by the opposite sex and must have sex only with the same anatomy as they are, in other words, an opposite sexual encounter would make them un-gay or bisexual (which is still gay) but that's another book. Please take a walk down this highway with me for a moment and let's see how great the world would become if every person born from this day forward was gay starting today. Let's say there were no doctor's interventions, with that said, every human knows that it's impossible for them to procreate without the help of a man's semen into the egg of a woman. In this world, all doctors have abandoned performing sperm injections and all nations in this theory labeled that practice a barbaric act performed by breeders, therefore, it was destroyed and outlawed.

I'm about to take you on a journey of a world where there

is no artificial insemination and no frozen embryos to plant inside women for future life. By the way, we are going to find out later in this chapter if gay men would have sex with a gay woman for the greater good, if they had to. So, let's explore some of the things that might take place if everybody was gay today; please use your own imagination as well.

I started writing this book on August 11, 2014. Hypothetically, this date marked the end of natural conception as we know it. I mean the hearts of all men were only to be loved by another man, and likewise, the woman couldn't stand to be touched by any man, consider that this mindset has taken over the whole world. "Hooray," everybody's gay!

There are about 7.2 billion people on the face of the earth today, and there are about 140 million babies being born every year, but August 2014, the last precious bundles of joy will arrive, and all of them will be born gay.

Hypothetically, starting today, we all are gay. Unfortunately, about 5 million newborn babies die in the first four or five months of their precious lives for various reasons. Doctors have tried to prevent intrapartum-related complications, asphyxia or lack of breathing problems, and birth defects to name a few causes. Over 300,000 women die giving birth every year and over 600,000 babies are aborted each year.

In the year of our Heavenly Father, August 2014, the last babies made it to earth. The United Nations would see no need for artificial insemination and outlaw all practices associated with it. In this world, it would be a SIN for gay people to act as the BREEDERS did. What's so bad about that? you might ask. Well, let's find out together, keep walking down this road with me to the "Theory of Non-Heterosexual Existence" please. One year later in August 2015, all one-year-old babies worldwide will be a spectacle to behold, "and boy" would they be getting held and kissed. I believe these one-year-old babies will be treated like rock stars. Posting on Instagram, Facebook, and other internet sites will break the internet. TV ads for baby clothing, shoes, and other baby products for toddlers', immediately sees the writing on the wall. Profits off these royal ones will be insane! The little darlings will rule the world on a whole other level. The world will be these babies' oysters. How can it not be? They're the last little cute ones.

In May 2016, they enter the terrible twos. At this point, things will appear to be normal in the world and not much has changed, except for the first time in history, no woman will be pregnant on earth. So, all the obstetricians, pediatricians, and some physicians will have to start closing their business and change their professions. Infant clothing stores will be facing closures, baby milk companies are preparing to close their doors, and all companies that promote good health for toddlers are adapting to the new world environment without the little ones to care for. However, about 55 million people die each year of incidents, accidents, and natural causes (not including war), so at this point, the earth will be around 110 million people lighter. I believe people will start to ponder that there's no one else after these two-year-old's bringing up the rear, and they may sigh and say, 'hum.' Lastly, for the first time in history, no population 'boom,' interesting.

Unfortunately, people can only live for 120 years on earth (Genesis 6:3). So, that brings us to the year 2017, alas the terrible twos are now three-year-old's and asking their parents many questions, you know the ones: why am I the youngest person on earth, why, why, but why daddy? When can I go to school like my big sister? Why, why, why? Why does my friend next door to us have two daddies and I have two mommies? Why, why, why? How come I have to eat this? Why, why, why? Kids, you got to love them; they crave knowledge and they're so inquisitive. Not much has changed on earth in the year 2017; however, the parties are going all night long at the clubs; the youth are having themselves a blast. No laws, no rules to stop them from being what they are; for them, the world is finally FUN.

In 2018, the kids are four; they have more freedom to move around and more time with their friends after kindergarten or after home-schooling from their parents or guardians. They just want to play with their friends and their toys mostly, and life will be grand for them. By this time, an interesting proclamation will be in discussion at the United Nations. The need for biological and nuclear weapons is being discussed, and how to dismantle them altogether. I believe this world will have no need for war. War posturing yes, some skirmishes yes.

Gay people are a lot of things in the mind of heterosexuals, but they prefer not to war with their own kind, instead, they rather reason with one another. Yeah, they will fight with one another and even kill one another, but not on a grand scale, especially in this world. Heterosexuals are all about that war. Why? Hum!

May 2019, the last five-year-old children will be preparing to complete kindergarten and getting ready for first grade. At this point, all hospitals specializing in caring for women during pregnancy and child-birth, and doctors providing care for newborns infants, the clinical trainers in midwifery and obstetrics, will be out of business forever. I believe the cost of living will be stagnant because supplies and demands will slow down dramatically. The world will begin to see the homeless, poor people, and people going hungry as an important cause to abolish. Also, the races will take a serious look at the meaning of all life and begin to heal old wounds caused by racism and groups of people that felt superior to others, I don't think they'll have a choice.

Alright, 2020 is finally here, and the six-year-old kids are off to first-grade elementary school. The parents that held back on pursuing their careers and dreams, are off to find work, not because they must, but because they're feeling a little uneasy and just want to do something to keep busy. But the kids are having a good time in school, learning and enjoying the company of friends. The world is a little lighter in population in the year 2020, about 335 million 300 thousand less than in 2014 But the older crowds are still partying hard and fast. They're finally free.

In the year 2021, a few hurricanes no one has ever seen before will hit the Pacific Ocean with devastating force, killing about 50,000 people and displacing over 1.2 million people. The whole world will mourn at the carnage. But after years of restoration, recovery, and care provided to those in need, the world will begin to settle down to normalcy again. I'm not prophesying that this will happen, hurricanes just happen and with that kind of force who can tame it? But the Almighty.

In August of 2021, graduation for first graders of elementary school will take place. This will be huge. I believe the news anchors will be out in full force for all graduations of schools around the country. It will become a ritual to cover school graduations from that time forward. Well, this is a significant year because at this point, all the companies making clothes for kids under five years old are shut down or trying to start new businesses that cater to older kids.

All the stores selling toys for babies are having problems staying afloat, they're refocusing their ideas for making new things for consumers, all the companies making infant and toddler products, pediatrician products and a host of other kids' products would start to vanish off the shelves. All the companies around the world catering to kids' products will have to lay off workers by the hundreds, if not by the thousands, depending on the size of the factories and companies providing services for kids. People are forced to reinvent themselves or retire.

The journey continues, the last six-year-old kids are about to graduate from first-grade elementary school. I remember my first day of school; I was both scared and excited at the same time, but other than that, I had no worries; how about you? Think back on your first day of elementary school. But these kids are different, not just because they were born gay, but because they are the last kids to attend first-grade elementary schools forever.

"And they know it," a male may boast, "I'm not like the breeders used to be. I'm proud of being gay, I don't want anything to do with penetrating a woman's vagina because inside of me, I am a woman. A female may proclaim, "I don't want no man putting his penis in me, besides, I'm not a breeder, which totally grosses me out."

I'm just pointing out that gay people don't have the same mindset in any way as heterosexuals do. Our perceptions of life are different. We don't wear the same type of clothing; we don't walk the same way; we don't react the same way to situations. We don't love the same things; our appearance isn't the same; we don't share our emotions alike; we don't think the same thoughts about life.

Since these fine folks are truly gay, there is no way in hell they should touch the opposite sex with a ten-foot pole, right? However, they could be bisexual, but again, we aren't talking about them; that's another book. Let's continue please…in the year 2021, the kids are seven years old entering second grade, elementary school preparing for the rest of their lives. Meanwhile, all the brick-and-mortar kindergarten schools are closed, people are losing their jobs at an alarming rate like never before recorded in history, despite living in a good economic environment; many food distribution companies are going out of business or changing their products to suit older people needs. School nurses and doctors are looking for work elsewhere, toy companies are going out of business, and all other major companies catering to kids are in big trouble or gone. No little cute baby pageants ever again; by the way, at this stage in the theory, the little kids' pageants are booming though, but a host of other companies like the little league sports are seeing some big changes and also filling the crunch.

Fast forward six years to the year 2027, these kids are thirteen-year-old "teenagers;" they'll be on their way to graduating middle school at this point, and all elementary schools are already closed. And all of those teachers, principals, coaches, cooks, curriculum book writers for younger kids, and any other groups associated with elementary schools, who made a living off the preservation and development of toddlers, little kids, and adolescents are hurting badly. Educators around the world must change their strategies to make a living. They have to reinvent themselves by learning another profession to remain relevant in this society because their profession has become obsolete.

I wonder what would be on the minds of the teenager. I can see it now, these vibrant young people marching onward, looking behind them, knowing that there's no one is coming up after them. They'll be the first generations without nieces, nephews, or any kids of their own to coach, share experiences with, or simply hang out with. No more, I'm going to be an uncle or an aunt soon. Meanwhile, all they see is elementary school after elementary school becoming a ghostly vacant relic. Then maybe they'll say in their hearts, "The breeders used to keep those schools full of heterosexuals back in the day, and almost all of them were people filled with contempt against gays, good riddance breeders."

Maybe that will bring some form of relief to the hearts of all gay people in some way, form, or fashion. It may finally show how good life could be without heterosexuals. They may think to themselves, if only the breeders would have just accepted us as we are and understood that we can't change the way we feel. Because gay people want heterosexuals to realize that they can't stop being gay because it is how they're made. Some have said, "If everyone would just try it, and don't knock it, this might be a better world to live in."

Maybe there's some truth to that notion, let's find out together. I'm focusing on the children because at this juncture, the adults are just working hard, playing hard, and giving into marriage or divorce or in the hospital being cared for. Mentally, I wonder how being a non-heterosexual would affect the psyche of people in this world; maybe they will just party like it's 1999 and say, "Forget about it, I'm doing me."

I wonder if gay doctors could convince gay people to set aside being gay to procreate once, just a thought. Let's get back to the scenario. The thirteen-year-old teenagers have graduated from middle school, and everything is going well. The next year, in 2028, they'll be 14-year-old freshmen in high school (depending on the age allowed in that district). Meanwhile, the older gay community is trying to figure out a way to live longer but to no avail; we as humans can only live (if Yah permits) 120 years of age, and that's providing armed forces in this new world have nothing to fight about, let's pretend not.

Well, as life continues on earth, people are still going to movies, watching various forms of theatrical entertainment like musical concerts, Broadway shows, football, baseball, basketball, racing, soccer, tennis, and many other activities that please men and women, fun is at its highest capacity. Although some entertainment in that new world will somehow be different; I can't quite put my finger on just how different it would look, but use your own imagination.

Just as it is today, so it will be in that day also. Disease will still be the number one killer of all mankind, and the doctors will gravitate toward the younger men and women to encourage these young minds to go into the medical field. It would be a mad dash to preserve life on earth because of what's looming on the horizon.

In the year 2028, the sophomore years are here, and all the students are looking for someone special to share life with. Training in various types of schools across the nation is intense, but the students are ready for it. I believe that the graduating classes across the world will see a rise in the number of graduating students ever recorded across the globe, which includes all the educating institutions from the Universities to the 9th grade. The youngest age on earth in the year of 2029 is 14 years of age. The 13-year-old kids and younger have been eradicated.

Although electricians, plumbers, steelworkers, carpenters, sanitation, engineers, and other professions is still the order of the day, there would be no profession that pays more or has better benefits and perks than the medical fields. It would be in such a high demand like no one has ever seen before. By then, I think that the world would have finally reached a solution on how to disarm and dismantle nuclear and biological weapons invented by the breeders safely. It would make front-page news, and the world will rejoice in its decision to destroy them.

Athletic coaches around the world will have to increase their knowledge from coaching ninth graders in high schools, to the college and professional level. This will be difficult because, in this world, the athletic coaching positions are becoming extinct or a terribly saturated field of occupation.

Eighteen years have passed since the last baby was born; that brings us to the year 2032. This is the year where things will begin to take its toll on the future of the gay society. The final high school graduation is front news everywhere around the globe, some 18-year-old young adults have their eyes set on not going to college, but still, for some of them, their attention would be toward enjoying life to the fullest.

Some will be forced by parents to go get their degree in the much-needed medical field, still, others will say, "Life is literally too short for all of that, so, I'm going my own way." You know the deal; you hear it all the time from young adults 'they know it all.'

High school football, basketball, soccer, even university pro ballers (yeah, I said it), including professional athletics will be on the verge of becoming lackluster by this time. But the music industry will be doing great. New growth in entertainment will spark a fuse and make people feel good for the moment. Big businesses will survive in most countries though. But alas, hunger and the poor people will finally get the attention they needed in the non- heterosexual period.

Because of the lack of demand and strain on the economy, food and shelter will be plentiful. Prices in the oil industry will drop dramatically, fuel price would be like it was in 1940s, and the cost of flights will be great again.

Vacation hot spots will be at an all-time high. The last of the high school graduate classes will take place in the year 2034 because of some students held back for various reasons. It would be the most spectacular high school event ever. You know as well as I know, that the last of any monumental event will be grandiose, especially this one.

There would be about 2 billion, 340 million babies not born since 2015. Out of those babies, about 90 million would not have made it past the first four or five months of their precious lives. By using the Ecology Global Network, we can calculate about 990 million people have died between 2014 and 2032 of diseases, accidents, weather-related incidents, and natural causes. Barring no wars between the nations had occurred. That leads me to this thought, in the year 2014, there were about 7.2 billion people accounted for on earth according to Worldometers calculations, and about 82 million people that would have been added to earth's population since 2014 thereafter, were not added. So, since about 55 million people die worldwide every year (keep in mind the death rate increases every year), you can multiply that by 18, which gives you roughly 990 million people having passed away, then subtract 990 million from 7.2 billion, which gives you roughly 6.0 billion people.

In the year 2032, in my Theory of Non-Heterosexual Existence, the earth's population will drop to about 6.010

billion people left on earth. By now, the young adults are getting ready for college, and they are eager to be on their own. Like any other young adult, the parents had full control over their lives up to the age of eighteen in most cases. So, they are ready to taste life on their own terms. By the year 2034, all high school properties are being remodeled for some other type of business, but still, some of them are being preserved for museums and landmarks. I believe at this point, there would be a health crisis underway because the number of elderly people will increase in poor health and will be as common as it is today.

It stands to reason that the healthcare field will require more attention than ever before because there will be a need for about 15 million health care professionals just in the US. So, they'll need numerous healthcare providers to keep things flowing smoothly. That's a lot of pressure on these young adults in this world. But still, some of the young people will prefer to just party hard.

I believe in this world; the military will lose about one-quarter of interest in people joining the armed forces nationwide.

Serving the elderly will be top priority; needless to say, almost all young adults at the universities and colleges will enter the medical field and stay for their doctorate, so that they can take care of the elderly. Obviously, some of the students will do only two years of college, because life will be way too precious to spend six to eight years in college. But the good news is that other young people will just want to have fun and take their chances on starting their own business. Still, others would see a great need to go into other important working fields like robotics, electronics, engineering, carpentry, electrical, automotive, farming, and aircraft tech, etc. Four years later, will take us to the year 2036.

In the year 2036, the census around the world would no longer be, where moms and dads wait out on the street corner with their children for that first bus ride to school; it is a thing of the past. No baby showers, kids' birthdays, first day of elementary school drop-off and pickup, no teaching teenagers how to drive, no little league athletics, no school athletic programs, no sweet sixteen parties, no elementary schools, middle school, or high school, no sending off your last child to universities or college institutions. These special moments will be lost forever, but they'll all be written as historical events.

One year later in 2037, according to the Theory of Non-Heterosexual Existence, the youngest person on earth will be twenty-three years young. A great age to reflect on what direction to take from here onward. They may not be willing to look backward; it doesn't make them feel good or happy. They'll forge ahead and try to discover a way to remain focus on the future. They'll feel that looking back could plunge them into deep depression, and even suicide. These are interesting days ahead for these 23-year-olds.

But they'll have to persevere through it, and of course, with the help and support of their parents, partners, and friends by their sides, they'll get through the hard days. One year later (2038), they'll be twenty-four and loving it, "finger snap." Because many of them have graduated from college and are eagerly anticipating helping the community get better, although some of them are already in a residency, some are just getting started outside of being schooled for the first time. After all, 2.703 billion people over the age of sixty-five is counting on them. That's a lot of pressure on these students, which wouldn't ordinarily be there if the breeders were still alive. Starting their new positions on the job is extremely exciting and challenging, they just want to make the world a better place to live in and trying to come up with a solution on how to prolong life.

Meanwhile, physicians and pharmaceutical companies, are on a mad dash to discover a miracle pill, or what's been forever called "the fountain of youth." Doctors and scientists in this world will soon discover that the challenges they are facing to achieve that elusive Holy Grail, is just as difficult and challenging as heterosexual doctors and scientists have faced before them. They all had succumbed to failure after failure to prolong life. Most humans don't yet realize that we all are going through the "valley of the shadow of death." The earth is that valley, and your life being not promised to you, is that shadow of death, where there is no fountain of youth and no cure for physical death. Let me remind you of something, from the time that we're born, we immediately started to get old (start dying). Because time, plus valley, equals death. Unless you are born again folks, the "Fountain of Youth" is being reborn in Yahuah.

Also, in the year 2038, almost all students are graduating; this graduation class will be very emotional. So, 2038 will be the greatest achievement of these students lives thus far. Their fears and excitement will overtake them, and their emotions will move the world to uncontrollable brokenness. But now the year 2039 is here, which means the final graduations in universities of higher learning in history. Needless to say, it will be a thing to witness, and it will be broadcasted over the airwaves of all communication devices known to humans. There are no emotions to describe the finality of that day. These are the last students ever to complete their residency, they are eager to take their place in society and start a new life with their partner. Five years later in 2044, the youngest person on earth is now 29 years old, now things are getting real and they're not liking what they see now.

They'll probably start to seek other gods to help them live a longer life or something. But they soon realized that one hundred and twenty years on earth is still the longest time given to mankind, whether you're gay or straight. Allow me to pause here for a moment. Straight is an interesting terminology used for heterosexuals, since straight is defined today as extending or moving uniformly in one direction only: without a curve or a bend. So, what does that say about any other lifestyle?

Back to 2044, I believe there will be so much pressure put on gay women to allow gay men to have sex with them. And gay men will be against it. Some will say, "After all, isn't it a disgustingly act amongst us since we both are gay?" But gay women will say, "Don't use me as a breeder because that's not who I am." Besides, it's our law not to engage in practices that are against our nature.

But you know politicians; the United Nations that had outlawed all artificial inseminations in 2014 will begin to take a good look at this ruling again in 2044. War will loom from one side of the united counsel that's for it, and rumors of war from the other sides who are against it. Debates and arguments will be fierce at the United Nations. For the first time since 2014, International peace, security, and gay people will feel threatened by their own gaydom. After 29 years of peace. War is looming.

Meanwhile, they'll continue doing whatever they choose to do with the time they have left on earth. Five years later, in 2049, the youngest person on earth will be thirty-four years old. The notion that a gay person doesn't need the opposite sex to survive will start to become a serious topic.

But when you're gay, how can such talks take root; how can you consider having sex with a gay woman if you're a gay man? And how, if you're a gay woman, can you consider having sex with a gay man. If you're gay, you can't stop being gay, that's the proclamation of gaydom is it not? But if you lived in this optimum gay world theoretically, and you say to your partners and friends, "Should we have sex with the opposite sex just until we replenish the earth and then stop." This can mean only one thing. A few lies were told to you by science, doctors, mainstream media, and lies you covered up just to convince yourself and others, which turned out to be FALSE. This is call "Pagan Culture" interwoven into our society.

Preferential sex is not a gene you're born with; sex isn't just sex. Therefore, sex is not the only thing that the gay community can point to, to prove that they're indeed gay.

How about love, can the gay community show the world that love has everything to do with being gay. I love my car, I love my dog, I love my job, I love my trips to special places around the world, I love making something out of nothing, I love music. Loving something does not equate to whom I have sex with because I can have sex with someone and not love them. Salah.

Lionel Riche said, "Love will find a way;" Bonnie Raitt said, "I can't make you love me if you don't;" Tina Turner said, "What's love got to do with it?;" The Spinners said, "It takes a fool to learn that love don't love no nobody;" The Isley Brothers said, "Love the one you're with;" Christians say, "God is Love;" followers of Yahweh say, "If you love Him, you will keep His commandments."

So, what is love? We know that love isn't exclusively just on earth. Someone might ask, "What do you mean teacher?" Well, first I'm perplexed that you asked.

And second, don't you know that there are two different types of love that matters, but only one that you should diligently seek after. The first one is a worldly or man-made love. This is the type of love that holds a lot of stipulations, restrictions, confusion, and confinement in relationships. Its foundation is based on many parameters. For instance, "You better keep making me feel special," "I'll continue to love you if you do this," or "I'll continue to love you if you don't do that," "Don't get fat," "Don't go broke," "You better keep me happy by buying me things," "I can have another you in a minute," and so on and so on.

If your love is based on the world or man's weak foundation, it's easy to walk away from and often will not last, that's why the same people that proclaim that they love you, are the same ones that will kill you, or tell you that they don't love you anymore. As surely as your lover sees fit, they will disappoint you time after time because the worldly or man-made love is flawed. It has way too many conditions, with no real permanent foundation. Also, it's common to find yourself saying, "the grass is greener on the other side" and fall out of love. How confusing is that? How can you fall out of love? Or is it that you really never loved? Or maybe you didn't know how to truly love?

Agape love is sure. Yahweh said, "Love your neighbor as yourself" and "Love your Elohim with all your heart and with all your soul." Yahweh said, "I love them that love me "Selah" and those that seek me early shall find me." Yahweh said, "Love cover up the multitude of sins." Yahweh said, "My love is everlasting." Yahweh said, "I will love them freely." Yahweh said, "My love will never fail," and lastly Yahweh said, "Love those who despitefully use you."

No matter what someone says or does to hurt you, you must forgive them and continue to love them even while you're separated from them. Must you accept what they said to hurt you? NO! Should you accept what they did to hurt you? NO! But work out the reasons why they hurt you, forgive them and continue to love them; this is the approach to Agape love.

We must seek this type of love while we're here on earth and achieve Agape love in the fullest there of when He returns. This type of love is the most expensive love a person can give because it takes the body, soul, and spirit for you to cultivate it. But it's also the most rewarding love you'll ever cultivate. How awesome is that? But Yahweh does hate evil people (Romans 1:3) and evil doers (wicked), Psalm 5:4-6,9-10). Please don't get Yahweh twisted.

This type of love has a sure solid foundation because it's not of this world, therefore, if you do or say something to someone to hurt them, you should ask them to forgive you and don't do it again. That's called repenting (Acts 3:1). Then continue in love without conditions or stipulations because they forgave you, and you have forgiven them.

Also, your heart is kept clean of resentment, clear of getting back at someone for that wrong thing they did to you. Your conscience will remain clear, and you can sleep well at night. No one can point at you for the collapse of the relationship, and you can walk away with your head up high, with a free disposition because there was no other way to reconciliation. Now that's a form of Agape love.

On the other hand, if a person says, "I love Yahweh and believe," although His love for you is sure, still, because you have not repented (stop sinning) and refused His will," He will tell you to depart from His sight (Matthew 7:21-23). What does this have to do with the Theory of Non-Heterosexual Existence? Everything! Because it proves that love doesn't equal who you have sex with, and earthly love can't get you into heaven.

Back to the year 2049, the youngest person at this time is thirty-four years old, and here are some of the things that I think will be the order of the day. The last universities and college graduates who completed their residency has gotten their doctorate. A huge celebration is happening for the students on the grandest scale of all times. The other graduating class who didn't go for their doctorate would have gone on with their life's years earlier. They're gainfully employed and are already living with their partner.

Work should be plentiful, and there should not be any homeless people on the face of the earth at this point because the nations finally got it right. Let's just say that there's peace on earth because there's more important things looming in the hearts of people in this world. Even more important than having his brother's possessions, more important than disease, more important than love, more important than hate, and more important than being gay. The name of that beast looming is the year 2134. But we'll get back to why this year is significant in a bit.

In this world, it doesn't seem that there will be no exemption from any businesses becoming extinct, for instance, at this point all employment related to education, construction workers, building maintenance, electricians, brick masons, people to keep grounds, and building equipment workers, will be hurting because of the shutdowns occurring, with no end in sight.

Teachers and professors of higher learning suffer a great collapse. Textbooks for the curriculums of higher education learning will be about 80% less than before. Some professors would be needed for refresher courses though. Nurses, and other medical services who provide aid to students, will likely enter the mainstream medical industry.

Companies that make fly gear for students are now making some other type of clothing, but it's not as lucrative as the fly gear of the past, and the competition for clothing contracts will be fierce because there will be approximately 5,275 billion people on earth in the year 2049, but about 60.2 percent of them is 65 to 91 years old. So, there are plenty of companies vying for big and small clothing contracts, and they'll soon realize that the field of garment makers are becoming saturated.

Work will be hard to come by because the landscape for finding new contracts has changed dramatically, many businesses will have their pick of the litter; there will be no rush for nothing in the clothing industry because the industry is doing well. The bosses are worry-free of paying too much for excellent contract terms. Contractors trying to keep their employees busy are finding that the employment field is plentiful. Yes, the economy is doing just fine in this hypothetical world, even better than the world we now live in.

But by the year 2057, the total world population will be around 4,535 billion. Every biological parent since 2014 will be between 61-78, providing they were between 18 to 35 years old when they gave birth in 2014, 61 years old if they were eighteen years old when they gave birth in 2014, or 78 years old if they gave birth at the age of 35 in 2014; so, you could see that the last of the biological parents are being phased out also.

The youngest person in 2057 will be 42 years old. They won't be doing what most forty-two-year-old people are doing today; at this age, there's no new professional sports games being played by the young. Gone are the days of the draft from colleges and universities, gone are the days rooting for your home team to win again, no play-offs coming, no divisional games to gear up for. Therefore, no championship games to cheer on and have parties for. No new baseball games to watch, no grand slams, no homerun hitting, and no walk-off plays to get excited about, and I can't wait to discuss it around the water cooler with your game buddies at work the day after the game. No world series for you and your crew to get ready for.

No new basketball dunking, three-point shooting, cross-over alley-oops to leave you in awe, no fade-away jump shots at the end of the buzzer to win the game, no leg-breaking double moves that left your opponent in the dust lay-ups.

No skating magic, hockey puck scoring, SCORE! SCORE! No, you just had to be there to believe what you had witnessed. No hard nose play by play punching your opponent on the ice, no getting sent to the cooler because one of your favorite players just had a fight with a 'bad man' from the other team. No more air horn blasting after your team just came back from being down a 3 to 1 deficit to win the trophy. No more awesome games like, "I'm glad I was there, front and center (at home watching TV) or at the stadium when the Americans took home the gold medal in the Olympic Hockey games against the Russians in 1980."

The only sports being seen is the networks that have reruns of all the greatest games of the past, these tracks will be treated like gold. Hollywood will have a great time producing gay films one hundred percent of the time. Gay soap opera will be the talk of the day at the water cooler. But more interesting than that is the looming fate of the gay gene toll on mankind causing a worldwide panic.

By the year 2067, food will be plentiful, and there will be no hunger anywhere on earth, and no homeless person either. All the buildings such as apartments, condos, rental homes, and homes that were vacated because the last family survivor died, will become a haven for the homeless.

Suddenly, paying outrageous prices for everyday items is a thing of the past.

The reason you won't have high prices in this world is simple, fewer people to supply goods and services to (except the medical field) such as water, food, gas, electricity, and oil. The lesser consumers, the less it costs to provide for them. All prices are rolled back to 1939. The mindset of these people will probably be, why let someone suffer and die unnecessarily when we need all people on earth to be in good health. The space program, however, will be suffering because of the lack of reasoning to colonize a planet in our galaxy. The program will turn to a deeper exploration of this planet instead. Money won't be a problem but annihilating diseases and living longer will take precedence over space exploration. They'll have to try to live longer than 120 years.

By the year 2077, the youngest person on earth will be 62 years old, can you imagine that? Among other problems, the animal world and insects will be a big problem for these people. Although they will have dominion over animals, the rate of increase by animals will no doubt be a problem. And it is at this point that the gay community will start to think thoughts along the lines of, 'If I live for 30 more years, how can I rely on the police, the doctors, the farmers, the builders, the medical ambulance, the fireman, the military or any emergency responders to help me? They all will be 92 years old. Even if I have the strength to help myself, if a tornado strikes, an earthquake happens, or a hurricane hits my area and knocks the power out?' What then?

'Who am I going to rely on then? And what can I do to help others when I turn 92 years old?' In every agency I just mentioned, employees will also be 62 years old or older. One may think, do I dare wish, that there were a few breeders left, but alas the gay gene has completely taken its toll.

They'll ponder, should I have sex with the opposite sex, just to procreate? And if I do, what am I? Why am I having such filthy thoughts about breaking my own belief concerning my sexuality? I cannot do this, because if we can do this, it would make every gay person a lie. And lastly, if we did this, wouldn't we have to continue doing this? Then what are we to be called? Gay Straight? Gay Breeders? What? It wouldn't make any sense.

Then the gay community will begin to graft hard on the operations of robotics, the robotic world will be extremely important to the gay community, and since there are no young people coming up after them, robots will become their best friends, housekeepers, policemen, firemen, medical responders, builders and everything in between. By the year 2097, people will be totally dependent on robots.

Problem-solving robots are running most of everything in the year 2097, but still, the gay community is faced with another challenge, and that is, how to be stronger, healthier, and live longer. Although we have made great strides in this category; we're still getting sicker and dying earlier than we would want to.

The problem we faced in 2014 would still be the same in the year 2097 with a few improvements of course. With these great advances, we now know more about our health concerns, the food we eat, and so on, but from a practical standpoint, we still have a long way to go. So, would this gay generation survive with the help of robots?

The year 2107 has arrived, and the youngest person on earth would be 92 years old. But first, let's do a short recap, in 2014 the elusive gay gene hit the earth's population and the population became stagnated at 7.2 billion people. In 2015, the babies turned one year old, so now is the year 2107, and they're 92 years old. About 55 million people die globally each year. (The rate accelerates each year). With that said, the world population would be around 2,140 billion in 2107. Selah.

At this time, let's just say humans have perfected humanitarian robots and incorporated it into everyday life. Robots will be harvesting food, doing medical research, tending to the elderly, delivering goods and services, building space crafts, sailing the open seas, flying aircraft, and dare I say, keeping dead people functioning because they'll replace the dead organs, and dead limbs with synthetic and titanium ones. They'll make you part of what they view your functional life should be, according to how they were programmed, keeping your body operating even though you died. That's what robots do; they keep things functional. "Don't think for one instant that this isn't already happening."

"The year 2133 has arrived" you see, the last few million humans are 120 years old, and all humans are in some form or care units on their death bed, they're being overseen by robots. according to the Theory of Non-Heterosexual Existence. The year 2133 marks the end of the gay lifestyle experiment, and consequently, the end of human life on earth as we know it. Because of no procreation, here is why life ended. No nuclear bombs were dropped, no World War III, no major diseased epidemic had to occur, no famine, no cataclysmic event took place, Elohim didn't come to destroy us for being disobedience. Every human just being gay wiped all of us out. So, ask yourself this simple question, what is the most excellent lifestyle that mankind can achieve?

Chapter Five

My Personal Thoughts

Philippians 4:8 "Finally, brethren, whatsoever things are true, whatsoever things are honest, whatsoever things are just, whatsoever things are pure, whatsoever things are lovely, what soever things are of good report; if there be any virtue, and if there be any praise, think on these things."

If gay people are right and we as heterosexuals are wrong about how we view a relationship within the confines of marriage, then let our lifestyle be a lie to all of mankind. Let all of mankind change to reflect and accept the gay lifestyle as being the more excellent lifestyle that mankind can ever achieve.

If both heterosexual and gay lifestyles are right, then let us recognize each other's existence and differences and go our separate ways, but let the people and government reflect the needs to concretely separate church morality from state immorality influences. All the branches of government shouldn't seek to take the rights of one group over another's rights and privileges, like they're doing today. But instead, mandate all righteous deeds and laws to allow both lifestyles to co-exist. Don't allow any corporations, person, or any entity to infringe upon the rights of one lifestyle over another by any court system.

If heterosexuality is a more excellent model for sexual preference in captivity, then let every government on the face of the earth acknowledge that fact, and let the whole world strive to become their best within that model. Likewise, let all synagogues, churches, and businesses reflect that notion without reservations or reprisals. Then let us cultivate it with all reverence of our people and our Heavenly Father.

But if the word of Yahweh is right and true, and all humans are wrong about the lifestyle that we live, then let us, as a nation, turn to what is written in the word of our Heavenly Father. Let all mankind conduct themselves in a sexual manner, according to His word; honor it, cultivate it, live righteously by it, be led in truth and let the Holy Spirit (the Ruach) become our teacher and start over again in righteousness. Let us reflect and honor Yahweh's design for mankind within the dignity of His designs for all humanity.

Let it be mandated in our schools, businesses, homes, synagogues, and churches. Let the government honor all laws and audiences of Yahuah (the Messiah) and rule with an iron statue against those who oppose Yahweh's laws. Because we must take great heed to what the Holy Scriptures said about what happens to people and their land that we possess because of wicked choices and lifestyle of immorality in their hearts. It happened before. It WILL happen again.

Question: If someone were to ask me, "Who are you?" My answer would be "I'm a child of The Most High 'Yahweh.'" If someone were to ask me, "What are you?" My answer would be "I'm a Hebrew male, a father, a son, an uncle." If someone were to ask me, "What do you do?" My answer would be "I go to work most days, where I'm considered to be a jack of all trades, master of none; I have sex with my wife, I have fun with my family, and sometimes I have bad times with my family and friends. I go to functions and events with my family and friends, I worship the Most High Yah, and I'm trying hard to love my neighbors as myself." What would your answers be to these questions?

Mystery of Hell

You see, who you are isn't what you do, therefore, being gay isn't who you are, it's what you do, being heterosexual isn't who you are, it's what you do. It's about whose seed (Spirit) you carry within, or flesh (iniquity) you carry "within." It is what determines who you are (John 3:3-8). So, if this is true, that means all the things that I do, I can stop doing them, including not serving the Most High Yah or Satan. But I'll still remain loved by Yah until I die. Because of the hardening of my heart towards Him, I die twice (Revelation 2:11), (Revelation 20:14). At that point, I just wouldn't be His child anymore and wouldn't (Matthew 7:23) enter the Kingdom of Heaven.

Then Hell becomes my portion because my name wasn't written in the book of life (Revelation 20:15). I chose to go there because obeying my Heavenly Father wasn't more important to me than the pleasures of this earth. He just gave me what I chose. Therefore, Yahweh didn't send you to hell. People on earth can't send you to hell; you sent yourself to hell. So, please stop being hateful and angry at Yahweh for giving you what you wanted.

About the Author

Vernon was born in Dallas, Texas, and he lived as a young man in Oak Cliff, Texas. He attended Wilmer-Hutchins High School and hated it with a passion. So, in 1973, by the guidance of his father and mother, Vernon sojourned to Sam Marcus, Texas, where he attended Gary Job Corps to study electrical and carpentry. Vernon graduated from Gary Job Corps in 1975 with his high school diploma and apprentice license in both electrical and carpentry.

Vernon worked at the Pascagoula Mississippi Shipyard until he entered the US Navy in 1977 as a Cryptologic Technician. He loved being in the Navy because he got to see the world in a real way, and got the chance to live in many places, the Philippines, Japan, California, and Florida.

After his tour with the Navy ended in 1983, he got married. Vernon now has three interesting children that keep him on his toes every day, and he loves them deeply. He worked in the window treatment business for a few companies. Vernon went back to school and acquired his associate degree in the electronic field from DeVry University in Irving, Texas.

After graduating, Vernon worked as a building engineer for many years. In 2011, he went to work in the oil field for Halliburton Energy as a tool technician. While working as a tool technician, Vernon received the inspiration to write this book, "Theory of Non-Heterosexual Existence." Vernon is so grateful to Yahweh, he lives by this gratitude mantra, "I owe my life to my Heavenly Father Yahweh because He guided me and protected me from gangs, jail, and dying before my time." Vernon's parents, Leo and Dora Watts, were great to Vernon and his siblings. They didn't have much, but what they had was shared with one another.

Although his parents are deceased, the family remains close and connected. As for Vernon today, he is in the real estate wholesale business, and he loves it.

Also, he is using his electronics skills to invent things.

NOTES

NOTES

NOTES

NOTES

NOTES

NOTES

NOTES

NOTES

NOTES

NOTES

NOTES

NOTES

NOTES

NOTES

NOTES

NOTES

NOTES

NOTES

NOTES

NOTES

NOTES

NOTES

NOTES

NOTES

NOTES

NOTES

NOTES

NOTES

NOTES

NOTES

NOTES

NOTES